OVERGRUWN

First published in 2025

ISBN: 978-0-9930813-9-2

Printed in the United Kingdom

OVERGROWN

AND OTHER POEMS

W.S. PENDRAY

Contents

Foreword by Dr Jess Moriarty
Principal Lecturer in Creative Writing
University of Brighton

"like an offering, like a gift

we never knew we needed"

dream 37 – Will Pendray

In one of the incredible poems in this anthology, Will gives a visceral description of the road near his childhood home, describing birds bursting into flames whilst smelling of incense. It strikes me that like much of his writing, he is using a detail from his lived experience to say something about the cultural and social world at large, and for me, the birds serve as a poignant metaphor for the world we find ourselves in. The world is burning. Like so many others, I started 2025 feeling aghast by the inauguration in the US that demonstrates how far the world has fallen, and the tight grip that the far right has on politics.

As I write, Trump has decreed that the

infamous Alcatraz Prison be reopened, and yet the media remains inert, unable to critique or challenge those in power. Watching the morning news is like looking into an abyss, but I am mesmerised by the awfulness and find it hard to look away. Everything seems hopeless and I feel my own desire to be socially active waning in the face of such a huge triumph for all that seems wrong with the world.

But in this heart-making and heart-breaking collection, Will reminds us that the arts are a way of highlighting the inequalities and horrors in the world whilst also magnifying the beauty that prevails within it. He shows us the wonder of nature, the birth of his daughter, the terrain of his own mental health and puts these up against a political backdrop generating frustration and despair. In doing so, he creates an intimate anthology that says something truly profound about the world today. The poems also offer us insights into Will's experience of incarceration and of how his creativity served as a scaffold, helping him to reflect on his time inside and also offering him means of mental and emotional escape. Will's writing shows us how the legal system in the UK ultimately lets everyone down. The poems raise awareness about the dehumanising aspects of prison life, and of how the current system only serves to perpetuate shame and violence in society. Will's poems are part of the crucial change we should all be hoping for. They are light reaching into the dark, making those places vivid to his readers and extending a plea for humanity at all costs.

Searing social critique, a celebration of nature, and a biography of Will's extraordinary life – but the anthology is somehow even more than this. Ultimately, *Overgrown* manages to be about love. It creates beauty where one might imagine there would be none, it celebrates the joy that Will finds in his loved ones and his lived experiences, and at its heart, it documents how the act of writing has helped Will to love himself again. And this is perhaps the most inspiring and important part of the book.

Read *Overgrown* once and then read it again, and again, and again. I am changed as a result of Will's stunning and staggering writing, it has put me in touch with what it is to be human, telling me that we can't just stare at the abyss, we have to do - and also connect with - the work that lifts us up and out of it. It's the gift I didn't know I needed. It's the gift we all need now.

Foreword by Rachel Billington OBE

Author and Associate Editor, Inside Time

Overgrown is a surprising collection of poetry. A great many of the poems deal with youth offending, poverty, prison, depression, alcoholism, and despair. Yet such is the magic of words that reading W. S. Pendray is not a depressing experience.

There are various reasons why this book is exhilarating, even mesmerising. But firstly, it is probably important to know that the author spent four years in prison.

This a poet who has lived his subject in the least romantic circumstances possible. On his release, and with the help of The Longford Trust, he studied at Brighton University for an MA in Creative Writing and was awarded a Distinction.

At the simplest level, *Overgrown* is a journey, starting with two childhood poems, *Are we in heaven?* describing a car crash though a child's eyes and *The Stone* about the seven-year-old boy throwing a stone through the window of a telephone kiosk and being arrested by police,

...The officer delivered me home like a bad takeaway.

This apt simile is an early hint at Pendray's gift for choosing memorable words.

After childhood we travel through the bars into prison, where The Young Offender's *...wings are clipped before they could stretch.*

Longer poems are interspersed by brief running commentaries,

...bars grip these bones tight/
but my soul slips through the gaps/ stars remain distant

The words say it all, the lows: ... *the compost heap of old worries...*

But the highs are always there, the hope that is told through images most often to do with nature or the moon, *the moon plants flowers in my chest...*

In the title poem Pendray describes a tomato plant which he has grown lovingly, being taken away by a prison officer, but instead of giving in to the sadness, he writes,

So the man grew too, / found roots within...

Nature is used over and over again, but always with new imagination. Similes abound, *...cut back the overgrown / vines of anxiety...*

This link with Nature means that the possibility of rebirth and regrowth is implicit in almost every poem.

When Pendray leaves the prison and starts a new life, poems like *Breathe, Resurrection,* and *Grateful* makes real the hope that has always been there. The moving poem about his baby is called *Flower Moon*, bringing together his two inspirations for freedom.

The cover picture of Pendray silhouetted against a moon, with flowers sprouting out of his hat is no accident.

I have read those poems often and know that they will be appreciated by everyone who enjoys good poetry, written with underplayed style and a touch of wit. But I also hope they will be read by men or women who can identify with W.S. Pendray's journey through dark years and, like him, find a way through to the stars, or maybe even the moon.

Preface

When the prison walls closed in, these poems gave me space to breathe.

What you take from them is yours. I hope you find something that resonates, a reminder that, even in the darkest moments, growth is always possible.

WSP

are we in heaven?

blood drips from my brother's knee,
matchbox cars scattered from the back seat,
the man who hit us
flew through the windscreen,
his light blue t-shirt, his jeans
already melting into the asphalt.

The claws of his Ford Escort
shattered, reaching
for something.

Mum hauls us from the wreckage,
the air thick with smoke,
the hiss of oil seeping into silence.

Death waits,
weighing what's left to salvage.

Our ears ring with the toll
of St. Mary's bells, each chime
pulling the sky down,
closer;

time flinched,
                then stopped.
We stood on the road's edge,

suspended
in white.

The tarmac,
a dragon's back,
scaled and sun-baked
stretched before us.

I look up.
My heart,
hammering against the walls
of my chest,

the clouds holding perfectly still
like they were waiting
to let us in.

the stone

when I was seven,
I launched a stone,
a pebble really,

that fractured
the fragile glass of the phone box
at the bottom of our street.

The two kids with me sprinted off,
took a hard left on Canons Road,
I fled too, playtime was over.

I drifted homeward,
in the long shadows of the afternoon,
glancing back to see blue lights

creeping over the horizon
next to Londis.
Panic hit me, a sharp slap.

So, I bolted down the nearest alley,
mouse heart thudding
like a tiny drum.

I watched them turn,
fingers pointing,
daggers aimed at me.

The police car rolled in,
a bloody tank,
while I shook in my Umbro shorts

and scuffed astro-turf boots.
The copper, in full black gear,
yanked me from my hiding place

and dropped me into the vast
back of the car,
the seat swallowed me whole.

I was seven for fuck's sake,
didn't mean to break nothing,
just a pebble no bigger than a peppercorn.

But there I sat,
crawling through the garages,
a slow death-march,

a procession of regret.
The officer delivered me home
like a bad takeaway,

and my dad forked out a tenner
for the shattered glass,
but I've been paying in guilt ever since.

Now here I am,
handcuffs pressing into my wrists,
prison van spinning me into nothing.

Remembering how easy it was
to throw a stone
and make a world fall apart.

sweatbox

bloated piss bag
rattling in a plastic
tomb. *How's it feel,*
no/ no-good thug?
like a pearl in the throat
of a clam snapped shut.

outside

cars clash like cymbals,
cliffs crumble into restless seas,
the cat's claws scratch the silence.
CCTV frames our lives:
humanity caught in the glare
of its own headlights.

Bombs scatter like withered leaves,
buildings burn, branches snap,
brittle as unkept
promises. Politicians pick sides,
like boys in a playground fight.

Flags flutter and satellites blink above
the shifting clouds.
Banks throw long shadows,
dark enough to swallow anyone.

A prize for peace, awarded to a man
with bloodied palms.
Power sips its morning tea in marble halls.
Doctors bury their fatigue; patients breathe in
the antiseptic air. In rain-soaked gardens black
petunias open
in defiance.

Laws shatter, lovers ache,
and the world, insistent, turns.
I stand here, this old dressing gown,
wrapped around me like yesterday's news.

Smoking tobacco to the roach,
watching rats scurry freely, gnawing
at whatever's left.

Keys rattle, time exhales.
I lay down these tired bones,
And dream of open fields, a sky
wide enough to hold everything we've lost.

bars & stars

bars grip these bones tight,
but my soul slips through the gaps,
stars remain distant.

offer

he came at me
with a razor in his hand
and anger in his eye.

The warrior in me rose,
no time to think,
just a stance
that might've made
a kung-fu master proud.

Then,
he cracked a grin:
Wanna borrow this? he said.
To shave that beard off.

And just like that,
violence folded
back into laughter.
But my guard stayed up.

In here, you learn
to laugh with your fists clenched.

carry on

moth
or wolf

fly
or flea

what crawls,
what claws

inside
of me,

my skin
is thick

my heart
a storm

I stitch
my wounds

and carry
on

into the grieving dark.

run

you   run   from   your   past,
                           your   past   runs   faster.

visitation

under the cold steel door,
down the landing,
past the hate and vacant stares,
through locks, bars,
razor-wire fencing,
and over the main gate,

floating away from
this twitching bag of bones and breath.

out,
over moonlit roads,
across a sleeping ocean
where I see my Mum
stirring a saucepan,
while shaping something else;
a future, a memory.

I see my brother laughing
at something only he can hear.
I nod, unseen.
I wish them well.

then I cross rivers,
and drift over concrete
that once called me home.

mind the gap

my mind's a tube map,
lines snaking everywhere: red, green, blue,
a tangle of routes, crossing
intersecting, some closed
for maintenance. Delays, signal failures,
no progress. I pace this carriage
a restless fox on the platform's edge,
always one stop
from where I need to be.

My thoughts jostle like rush hour trains
breathless, endless
hustle of bodies, noise
never stops: rattling, shuddering,
doors that never open. Eyes
darting, hunting for patterns
in the chaos, but all I get is lost.

There's no way out. The map's
in my head, my head's
in the map. When the train
halts, it's just me, boxed in
these blank walls.

desert flower

I bloom
where mirages
fade.

Rooted in dust, twisting
through the dry,
cracked earth,

petals stretch through sand
thirsting for drops
of an unforgiving sun.

Rain never comes, salt streaks
my face, each line etched with waiting.
You wait for freedom.

Each day, we sip
from the cup of dreams
left to sour.

when night wraps
its heavy arms around us,
we bloom in the dark.

dream 37

birds were bursting into flames
at the bottom of the alleyway
near my mum's old house,
where the bricks sweat
cigarette tar and grease. The air tasted like
Supermalt and damp leaves,
I saw fat Matt down the cul-de-sac,
that black hole of our youth,
where we rode our bikes
until the sun clocked out
and the streetlights flickered on.

He was upset, heavier than before, I tried to
console him,
thinking his mum had passed, so,
I told him about my dad,
how cancer crept in
like a tenant we didn't know had a key.
We walked, our footsteps cracking open

the same concrete we stomped on as kids,
our old playground now overrun by saplings

too stubborn to stay underground.
I noticed how the weeds conquered
everything: tarmac, bricks, even us.

But this morning, when the walls returned
and reality punched its way through
I realised it was fat Matt who had died.

And the birds were still burning,
but now they smelled like incense,
like an offering, like a gift
we never knew we needed.

drunken moon

I sit alone in the dark,
   a moth lost,
      wings battered
         against the cold,
  empty face of night,

  anger, frustration
     ripping through my ribcage.

         Each thought scrapes
      like a rusty nail
    through the tender flesh
of memory.

Until the moon,
           drunken
       and laughing,
          spills itself
              across the
                   cell walls.

Serenity curls inside me,
      a flower too wild to name,
             its petals like fire

refusing to die in the rain,

      and for a moment,

     I'm free.

cake n' custard

I've ordered cake n' custard
for your birthday as a treat;
every time I say those words,
it's your voice I hear repeat.

You say, *watch'a* to the waitress
who glides across the sea
of checkered shirts and braces,
dirty plates and cups of tea.

An oasis for the truckers
on the dusty road of life,
I hear the nozzle splutter
in the quarry of my mind.

I close my eyes, imagining
my childhood in a bowl,
a steel spoon clatters,
chocolate sponge inside my skull.

Cake for men, proper stuff!
no fairy cakes, no la-de-da;
in truckers' caffs, proper gaffs,
no suave-lit, smarmy bar.

Sugar pots on gingham cloth,
bacon, beans, and diesel;
overwhelmed, I'm welling up,
tears crawl, slow as treacle.

I've ordered cake n' custard
for your birthday as a treat,
but there's no one here to share it
no one here, except for me.

remnants

locked in a box
I comb through the remnants
of who I once was.

brave up

before we were hustled
for the dreams of our youth,
we lived in the moment.
Wildflowers towered above
our outstretched arms, and the river's current
pulled us through days. The sun
poured its golden soup into the valley,
and time, once bent its knees to let us pass.

Each solstice sees the seasons shift and fade,
and now there ain't a sunset here to see.
These four walls shove my soul into the shade,
handcuffed beside your grave, the roses free.
I've cried enough; no more tears can fall,
you told me I should *brave up*, after all.

grow again

buried in dirt
I have learned to grow again,
the moon watches close.

coeur de lion

I walk between worlds
of both man, and beast,

wounded by the hunter's snare,
falling fast, unaware.

Scattered seeds where home once stood,
fields of youth, now gone for good.

Carcasses of rotting dreams,
on the wing, the vultures scream.

Weak hearts here begin fade,
what seemed a year was just a day.

Cry those tears or even blood,
tears will not make time erode.

When you feel you can't go on,
remember you're still standing strong.

Suffer loss but not defeat,
wisdom waits beyond your grief.

Walls and cells, your world is more,
let them hear your spirit roar.

grief alchemy

I speak from the soul,
it bleeds out of me, grief flows
into gold.

the universe

we're the universe,
tripping over its own feet,
clumsy, broken, and beautiful,
like a sunset bleeding
over fences built to keep us in.

growing up poor

if you grow up poor,
you learn to fight,
knuckles
speaking the language of concrete,
fists like two tiny islands
afraid of drowning.

If you grow up rich,
you learn to pay
someone else to throw the punch,
to pass the bruises on
like heir looms.

Your hands stay clean,
but, oh, how heavy they are
with all the things
you've never held.

graft

we graft for the pound,
the pound grafts us into the ground.

anchored

at eighteen we graduate from park benches,
sinking a couple in-between
strolling in the bar entrance,
as if there's something in our jeans.

This is what we inherit
from old men in checkered shirts,
and their father's father before them,
oh no, we are not the first.

Sorrows drowned in seas of amber,
drifting from emotion.
For grief, or stress, or happiness,
we've learned to crack another open.

We drink 'cause we have problems
we have problems 'cause we drink.
The old woman's on the warpath
she drove Bacchus to the brink.

The epidural's wearing off
give her gin instead.
For twenty fucking years
the old man's wet the baby's head.

The children are the future,
and boy they grow up fast.
From the cradle to the boozer
we stay anchored to the past.

downpour

have your little downpour,
unharness the tide of your emotion,
shield it from the slow burn of their stares.

You were meant to hold back,
gripping rusted shovels,
clearing grit from weary eyes,

never destined to be
more than a mound of rain-soaked earth.
But granite sleeps in your bones.

Those tears
you buried in dreams
we built from fragments,

and still,
the warm scent of wildflowers
lingers through the fractures.

tea diem

fresh summer mountains,
wrapped in soothing cloud,
where those fragrant leaves danced
on jade hills beyond the grey grind
of city streets.

In ancient fields, songs
of dynasties and fallen empires
poured through meadows, seeped
from fertile springs,
across oceans, your final voyage
traded for this:

plucked from glory, now
discounted on special offer,
bathed in the brief glow of shelf-less fame
in my seasoned China cup.

You once held empires in your veins,
now you bleed amber warmth into water.

Drained.
Your sorry remains
slugged into the blackness
of a plastic bin.

against the odds

the tip came like a whisper
in a smoky room,
fifty grand slid across the table,
smoother than sin,
an old-school grin, a smirk
carved in shadows
a dead cert! he hissed,
6-1, that horse is gonna fly.

The runner ain't so sure,
eyes flickering with doubt,
horse sense tingling,
holding the money like a lead saddle
he paced the paddock, calculating
shadows and stats,
smelling the track's sweat, and hay.

Instead, he bets on the favourite,
steady and sure,
then breaks from the gate,
gallops off into a day drowning in booze,
the sharp sting of cocaine
whipping him faster,
visons of phantom fortunes blurring
his mind.

Midday swirls into midnight,
lights and sounds merge into one.
The city's an unforgiving crowd, a stampede of
voices, hungry and wild.

He staggers, spent,
thinking he's fifty grand up,
until the phone rings
and slices through his delirium:

I knew it, I fucking knew it!
a shout echoes
hollow in his chest.
A runner thrown from his stride.
the dark horse flew, final furlongs devoured
under hooves of fire.

Now, his heart sinks
a stone in a tar-black sea,
three hundred and fifty grand down,
boss's shadow looming
along the homestretch of regret.

If you're going to dance with fate
you don't hold back, you charge,
you thunder through dark
with eyes wide, baring teeth,
no half measures, straight to the finish line,
to the bleeding, blazing
end.

still free

locked away, still free
in the quiet I find peace
the moon plants flowers in my chest

broken

letters scattered in the yard,
an *r* rolls in the dust,
the *k* splits the pages of a poetry book,
the *e* clings to the door,
its chipped paint peeling.

I pick them up,
stack them on my bunk,
and spell my name again,
only louder this time.

overgrown

I grew a plant from one tomato slice
found in the servery salad, never thought
it'd grow. It reached so tall,
with leaves that craved the light.
Each day I watered it, drinking every drop;
it thanked me quietly. Most nights, we'd sit,
and watch the T.V, read letters, our shadows
flickering on walls.
When the screws

came to take it away, they were sorry.
The officer I'd argued with complained
to the governor about my tomato plant.

They said it came from the top,
brought in vermin, had to take it, no choice,
they said.

So, the man grew too,
found roots within.

I began nurturing anything I could;
hair wild, uncut,
fennel from Indian spice,
chillies, petunias, roses
blossomed into limbs,

sunflowers stretched
              up
                to touch the sky.

Everything thrived.
I stole earth from the yard,
planting more seeds,

until my cell became a lush,
green forest,
overgrown with life.

jobs to do in the garden

first, rake up all the fallen
leaves of yesterday's mess, each one
a memory brittle and brown.
Gently gather them
before the new ones

have chance to fall.

Cut back the overgrown vines of anxiety,
before they suffocate your peace.
Carefully deadhead the dahlias,
and those not-so-sweet Williams.
Lay them to rest on the compost
heap of old worries, let the wind take

what it wants.

Too caught up scaling mountains
of metaphor, you often overlook
the small hills quietly growing
on the lawn. Aerate the tired
soil when the morning dew has lifted.
Let the ground gulp
air, let it sigh.

Rescue the black roses
and petunias from the cold
shade, before they fade
into dust. Weed out the fears
with patient hands. Mulch the past

with care, in the hope
that something new will grow
tender and defiant.

And for that old apple tree stump
your dad planted: make it a throne
for reflection, or a pedestal
for new dreams.

Take the watering can, holed and leaking,
fill it with your tears and soak the soil
of last year's sadness. Nurture it,

until it blossoms
into something real
this time.

spirit

even when I was pushing a broom,
sweeping yesterday's regrets off concrete,
or scrubbing the floors of public toilets
down at the marina, where salt air tangled
with the stench of bleach and my hangover.

Even when I bled,
in cages or gutters,
mistreated by officers and bosses,
another love gone like a sunset.

Even after all the fights,
knuckles split like ripe fruit,
handcuffs that never fit right,
hospital beds where I learned the lullaby
of my own breath,

there was always something
raging inside me,
an ember under all that ash,
a fire that wouldn't die
no matter how many gallons
of alcohol I poured over it.

I called it spirit;
they have another name for it now.

punk

my mind is a punk,
a riot in leather and spikes,
moshing through the order,
thrashing against the system.

I tell it to be quiet,
it sticks up two fingers,
spewing defiance
all over the silence.

the poor poet

they found time to complete a master's,
and stack various degrees,
while the poor poet, the wretched bastard
crawls on calloused knees.

They float on plump inheritance
in mansions plush and grand,
while the penniless poet earns a pittance
grovelling in the sand.

They bask in life's soft privilege
with endless time to write,
while the hungry poet's hollow fridge
mocks him every fucking night.

They dine on gilded platters,
sip from glass that's crystal clear,
while the weary poet's empty stomach
shatters hope year after year.

They scribble on perfumed pages
with quills of peacock plume,
while the tired poet hunts for sparks
in cold, damp, dim-lit rooms.

And still, they mock his language,
the roughness of his speech,
while the poor poet, on the verge of breaking,
finds his pen runs out of ink.

how to cook a tory

a favourite recipe for those who blow their money on fags, booze and non-essentials.[1]

Ingredients:
1 tory (ethically sourced if possible)
1 decade of austerity
1 dollop of privilege
1 tbsp. of sleaze
1 tbsp. salt
a splash of inequality
a pinch of broken pledges
1 wheat biscuit (supermarket own brand).
1 measure of indifference
1 tbsp. of scandal
1 knob of full fat conservatism

Method:
1. Take your ethically sourced tory
and extract a dollop of privilege
with a silver spoon.

Carefully peel away the remaining façade
of empathy. Place the tory on a large roasting
tray and season generously with salt
(rub it deep into working-class wounds for
maximum flavour).

Add a pinch of broken pledges.

2. Preheat oven to a low value degree[2]
(gas mark 2010) and grill until soft

and golden around edges.
For best results keep grilling until edges have
turned brown, faintly scabby
in appearance and in texture.[3]

3. Roll out the decade of austerity into a thin
sheet, enough to wrap the whole mess.
Sprinkle sleaze liberally over the top, drizzle
with scandal, and pour in a splash of
inequality. Crumble in the supermarket
own-brand wheat biscuit for good measure.

4. Remove the tory from the oven. Let it cool
on the rack of public approval. Take a well-
earned fag break, light one up and switch on
Sky News until the thick aroma of integrity
evaporates.[4] Enjoy a measure of indifference;
straight up, no ice.

5. Serve with a knob of full-fat conservatism,
and garnish with a dash of hollow rhetoric.
Serves 8 but may leave a bitter taste
for generations.

the apple

his story is my story,
funny how history repeats.

On Christmases and birthdays
when I can only call to say
sorry for the lack of presence,
hope you're happy with the presents.

The apple never falls far from the tree
as we know, so those seeds we sow
we won't see grow, while these leaves blow
more absence we bestow

as we become fathers fathering further away.
A soft touch who finds it hard to speak
when asked *Daddy when you coming home*?
Now the questions I once asked
are asked of me.

Proper dad seems condescending
now that we lack consensus,
another con sat in contact centres.

How do we make changes,
when the ones who never raised us
became strangers?

May this apple not rot
but, root, grow, blossom, and fruit
so, the next generation
can take a leaf from our book

to ensure our son's and daughter's paths
are not torn and marred
by every storm that passes.

We must applaud examples
of those, who despite hardship,
grew tall and walked through darkness,
in the orchard of absent fathers.

His story is my story,
funny how history repeats.

getting out

getting out was a letdown.

No welcome home banners,
just grey clouds hanging like tired flags.
People I knew; gone or ghosts,

aged and worn, worry etched in their eyes.
Panic climbs my chest, just trying to function;
each breath
an assault on my lungs.

The post office used to be a sanctuary
of normality, but now it's a warzone
of change. A grey-haired man in front,
short, angry, skin sagging
from his elbows like melted wax. He doesn't
turn, just snaps
tells me I'm too close, get back.
When it's my turn,
the woman behind the glass
gives me a look,
her eyes saying what her mouth won't.
I withdraw cash like it's 2015,
and fought back tears
when my fingers touch the plastic notes.

Electric scooters buzz like angry hornets,
people rushing, desperate,
as though the town's on fire
and no one bothered to tell me.

In Nando's, I'm swallowed by solitude.

The waiter, just a kid,
guides me past families laughing,
couples basking in citrus bliss.
I sit where I'm instructed
as if I wasn't a storm inside,
my stomach throwing punches.

QR codes mock me.
I just want chicken, something real,
something that tastes like the old world.
I linger by the sauce station,
fingers brushing bottles,
each flavour a path I could've taken.
The air bites, metallic,
like breathing in rust.
My feet, unsure on the concrete
of St. Michaels Street,
dance for the rhythm of routine,
but the beat's changed,
the old steps no longer fit.

Freedom tastes strange.
Bitter-sweet, past and now.
And here's me,
a prisoner of both,
trying to navigate this wasteland,
one uncertain step at a time.

freedom

freedom costs nothing,
nothing is what they gave us for free.

grief's got a waiting room

grief's got a waiting room
beige walls, no clocks, magazines
from the year you last felt alright.

there's no door out, just
a hatch where they call your name
when it's your turn to fall apart.

you can lose everything:
your mates, your job, the keys
to a house that doesn't miss you.

doesn't mean you're finished;
just means you get a ticket.
take a seat; the chairs are made of sighs,

the tea tastes of Tuesdays,
and the vending machine is filled
with old habits.

If you slum it there long enough,
you'll start to hear it: the kind of wisdom
they never taught you in school.

there was nothing

there was nothing,
nothing gritty,
nothing sore,
just honeyed words
from soft, privileged hands.

I needed more.
Where were the broken?
the bruised,
whose voices ignite the cold embers
of evening?

I found nothing,
so I sat down,
tea cooling into silence on the table,
its steam curling, twisting upward,
like questions no one dared to ask.

I began writing,
wondering,
does anyone else feel this emptiness?
maybe I'll stagger back into the blur,
past salt-bitten walls,
streets pulsing with neon,
bass throbbing in my bones,
to see if the chaos on these stony shores
still feels like life.

clay

throw me down
against the blackened surface,
shape me.

Run your fingers
over the coldness of my earth,
mould me.

I can be both:
obedient,
and resilient.

Pour your hollow sky
into the vessel of my chest,
let it burst like stars,

weightless in the space
where my heartbeat
used to be.

breathe

panic
grips me,
steals my breath,
I don't own it
anymore.

Pieces of myself
scattered,
fractured,
left in fragments.

Inhale:
razor wire,
hysteria ripping
through my bones.

Years of this,
thrashed into
submission,
not quite giving in.

Breathe.
A hit of spring air,
filling my lungs,
breathe again
slowly,
softly.

Exhale, let life erupt.
Soul spilling into endless sky,

seeping into soil,
into all I stand for.

I can breathe,
I can breathe
again.

over the hill

heavy step,
light breath
sky blushes.

Horizons stretch,
not with hope,
but with the weight
of quiet understanding.

Breath steadies.
The sky unfolds,
a letter from a life before mine,
unaddressed.

A still pause.
The world shrinks.
Heart waits.

Air cool on skin,
hand parts the wind,
shadows deepen and curl.

Letting go,
rolling down,
I breathe in what's left of the sky.

smile
each morning brings its reasons to smile.

the resurrection

dust the charcoal from your feet,
the world still burns.
You wash your hands clean,
but the smoke still clings to your skin.
Somehow,
you silenced hate.

The stone walls that caged you
are now the gravel in your throat.

Your heart?
your heart is a skylark,
beating against the grey,
soaring toward a sequined ocean
where light fractures like diamonds

over the poor man's river,
meeting the wealth of the sea.

silent rebellion

it started small.
Defacing faces,
scribbling moustaches,
blackening teeth
as if we could draw out the lies,
make them human again.

Then it grew.
Conformity was a garden
I refused to tend.
No TV license,
turning off evening news.
No ticking boxes.
Never voted.
Not for them.
A silent protest against the noise
of promises that sprouted
but never blossomed.

Unsubscribing
from junk mail,
friendships too.
finding freedom
in the empty spaces.

We hoarded rainwater
in old buckets,
grew tomatoes on windowsills
roots tangled in soil,
each leaf a small, green uprising.

What started as a hobby
became habit,
a necessity,
life.

A commune, not by choice.
Our circle, small.

Then came nights by the fire,
conversations sparked in the warmth,
tea brewing, steam mingling with smoke,
a full-blown revolution,
not loud
not brash,
but a slow, simmering quiet,
the kind that turns into thunder
when the storm breaks,
when the first raindrop falls,
and all is washed clean,
ready to begin again.

grateful

I forget to be grateful
lost in the shuffle of bills, debts,
high-rise piles of washing.

I forget to be grateful
amidst the deadlines, broken sleep,
the spin cycle of everyday noise.

But then,
between the hum of the fridge,
and the shuffle of feet on tired floors,

you say one word,
and suddenly,
I remember:

how morning light breaks through curtains,
how your voice can turn a room
into a home.

flower moon

the moon is a flower tonight,
just like it was
a year ago,

when you showed up,
seedling fists clenched,
ready to take on the world.

The streets are full of noise,
but we don't care.
We are rooted in the quiet
underneath the sky.

The flower moon, heavy,
watches over us, its petals unfurling,
lighting up the dark
with its silent bloom.

You and your mum drift off,
wrapped in its silvery glow,
while a thousand lotus flowers
ripple softly above.

I think of your first year;
the moment I prayed to your grandad,
wishing you would take your first breath,
to the joy of watching you grow,
hands full of daises,
offering them with a smile,
like you've always known
how to heal what's broke

You're part of this magic,

as the moon fades,
and the earth pulls you in
you will move through them,
as wild as the roots that break the stone,
always you, always free.

brighton beach, last night

It's strange, isn't it? how you can sit here
on the stones at midnight, a Guinness sweating in
your hand,

the smoke from a joint curling
like it's trying to escape,
and still feel
well, let's just say, alive for now.

You tossed pebbles into the waves.
The moon gave them a stage,
each little stone winking out with a plunk.

and there we were,
knowing my time was up,
the judge's gavel waiting somewhere in a room
with black coffee and heavy curtains.

Today I came back.
The same Brighton beach, the same stones.
The sea wide open and laughing at me,
as if to say *what now?*

And I didn't have an answer.
A seagull screamed my name.
It startled me,
but it wasn't you; just another local
looking for scraps.

I caught my face reflected in my phone screen,
a little older, a little rougher,

like the tide had dragged me back in for one
last round.

And later, I was on the train
passing farmer's fields,
and the gulls again, lined up,
sipping from the earth like polite guests
at a dinner party.

Maybe this is how we let things go:
we return to the scene, we try to walk
on the stones, we hear the gulls
and think of you,

but we don't cry.
Instead, we let the tide wash it out
not away, just out.
And ain't that enough?

dear young offender,

I know you're angry,
the world won't listen.
Your dreams: caged,
wings clipped before they could stretch.
But, it's you who holds the keys.

Forget what people think.
Their words, noise.
Background hums, never holding weight.
Integrity? hold that.
Crime's a dead-end street,
with no view at the end.

The odds are stacked like bricks,
to keep you out.
But you, you carve your name in stone, son.
Make it something they can't erase.

The system was built to bury us,
the 'lower class,'
the wounded.

Court papers inked in a language that ain't
ours, not to teach, but to trap.
Loyalty, it's a delicate

thing. Hold it close like a rose,
but mind out for the thorns.
Not everyone blooms forever.

When the blue lights flash,
don't run from fear:
run 'cause you've got somewhere to be,
a place the light still reaches.

Read like you're stealing,
write like it's your only breath,
keep dreaming.
You're a poet.
You're an artist.
The world doesn't see it yet,
but you are more than what they say.
You are loved.
You are important.
One day, you'll see it too.

And when you do,
you'll stand on the other side of all this,
feeling the weight of how far we've come.
The sun will feel different on your skin,
and you'll see it, in the eyes of someone who
feels like home.
You'll know then, you didn't just survive.
You lived.

The pain will heal, I promise,
and the scars? they'll be stories,
maps of where you've been,
where you've fought,
and where you've won.

So keep going, mate.
You'll be alright,

Will

Notes: verbatim Tory excerpts

[1]Lee Anderson on foodbanks (2023)
[2] Rishi Sunak on LBC on July 17, 2023
[3]Boris Johnson's Recipe for Cheese on Toast (*Corridors of Flour Recipe Book)* 2021
[4] Lee Anderson on Foodbanks (2023)

About the Author

Will Scott Pendray began writing poetry as a child, following in the footsteps of both his grandfathers. While serving an eight-year prison sentence, he started a BA (Hons) in English Language and Literature with the Open University. He recently completed an MA in Creative Writing at the University of Brighton, graduating with distinction. *Overgrown* is his debut poetry collection.

Printed in Dunstable, United Kingdom